A Highway for the Ages

❖

History's Amazing Cloth

❖

Hunza: The Land That Time Forgot

❖

Building a 21st-Century Silk Road

FOUR INFORMATIONAL TEXTS ABOUT THE SILK ROAD

by Jeanette Leardi

Table of Contents

Informational Texts

What is an informational text?

Informational text is nonfiction text that presents information in an accurate and organized way. It is often about a single subject such as an event or time period in history or a scientific discovery. It may be about any topic, such as a sport or a hobby. The research report that you write for a school assignment is an informational text. An article you read in your favorite fashion magazine or on a Web site is an informational text, too. A newspaper account of a local election and a history book chapter on a famous battle are additional examples of informational texts.

What is the purpose of informational texts?

Informational text has one main purpose: to inform. The best informational writing does this in a way that keeps readers' attention. It pulls readers in, making them want to keep reading and to know more about the topic.

How do you read an informational text?

When you read informational text, look for facts and for the details that support them. Read critically to make sure conclusions make sense. If there is more than one way to look at an event or situation, make sure it is given. Ask questions: *Did I learn something new from this text? Do I want to know more about it? Can I draw my own conclusions from what I have read?*

The text has a strong beginning that hooks the reader.

The information is accurate and the facts have been checked.

The text has a strong ending that keeps readers thinking.

Features of an Informational Text

The text uses primary sources when appropriate.

The text includes multiple perspectives so that the reader can draw his or her own conclusions.

The text has a logical organization of major concepts.

The information includes graphics that support the text.

Who writes informational texts?

Writers who know their topic well write good informational text. They do this by becoming mini-experts on the subjects they are writing about. They make sure that they support the information in their work with historical facts, scientific data, graphics like time lines and diagrams, and expert evidence. They provide more than one person's point of view. They use primary sources, firsthand information like journals and photographs.

3

Tools for Readers and Writers

Strong Lead

Writers of informational texts try to hook readers, or grab their attention, with the first few sentences, or lead. A strong lead tells readers something important about the subject and hints at what readers may learn. Writers use two types of leads.

- Direct lead—tells who or what the piece is about and why the subject is important

- Indirect lead—may quote someone, ask a question, describe a setting, or tell an anecdote, or true story, about the subject

Pay careful attention to the lead. Which type hooks you? Direct or indirect? The type of lead you prefer to read may be the type of lead you prefer to use in your own writing.

Word Origins

Where do English words come from? Did someone wake up one morning and decide to call that thing that takes your temperature a thermometer? No. Most English words come from other languages such as Greek, Latin, German, and French, to name a few.

Look at the word "thermometer." Thermo (*thermon*) is Greek for "hot" and meter (*metron*) is Greek for "measure." If you know what "thermo" means in one word, you can transfer that information to an unknown word and build your vocabulary.

Draw Conclusions

A good writer does not tell readers what to think about information presented in an article. Instead, she intends for readers to think about the "big idea" presented in the text and draw conclusions based on personal experience and evidence stated in the text. Conclusions are usually drawn after reading a large chunk of text such as a chapter, several chapters, or a complete book. They are also based on several pieces of information (at least three or four). Different readers might draw different conclusions from the same information.

About the Silk Road

The Silk Road was a 7,000-mile (11,000-kilometer) network of paths and roads across Asia, the Middle East, and Europe that formed the world's major overland trade route. Beginning in the second century B.C.E., thousands of merchants, soldiers, and religious pilgrims traveled the great East–West trading route. It began in China and stretched all the way to Rome. It was named for the most precious item carried on its route—silk.

This hand-colored woodcut from the Middle Ages shows merchandise being transported across the great Silk Road.

For centuries the Silk Road was the only direct link between the East and the West. Then, in the fifteenth century, European explorers decided to look for faster ways to move goods between the Mediterranean Sea and China. They soon found waterways that cut travel time from a year to a few months.

Traveling by sea was not without problems. Tradesmen had to worry about severe storms and attacks from pirates. Even so, sea travel gradually became the major way to travel between the East and West. Over time, for many reasons, the Silk Road became obsolete.

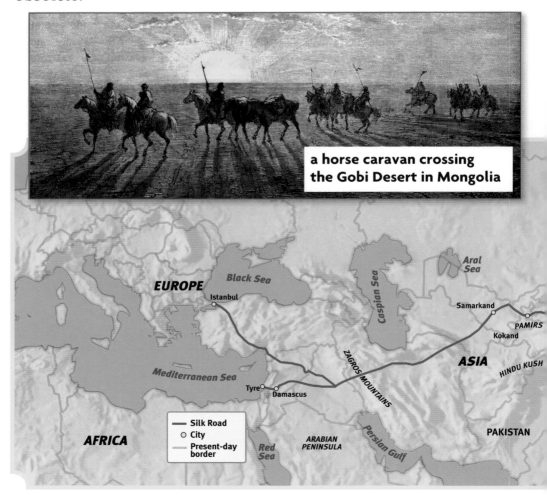

a horse caravan crossing the Gobi Desert in Mongolia

EUROPE

Black Sea

Istanbul

Caspian Sea

Aral Sea

Samarkand

PAMIRS

Kokand

ASIA

HINDU KUSH

Mediterranean Sea

Tyre
Damascus

ZAGROS MOUNTAINS

AFRICA

— Silk Road
○ City
— Present-day border

Red Sea

ARABIAN PENINSULA

Persian Gulf

PAKISTAN

Remnants of the road exist today. Some cultures unaffected by the passage of time, like the Hunzakut, live along its paths in northern Pakistan. Now, a thirty-two-nation Asian Highway project is underway. When completed, it will be a modern version of the great Silk Road.

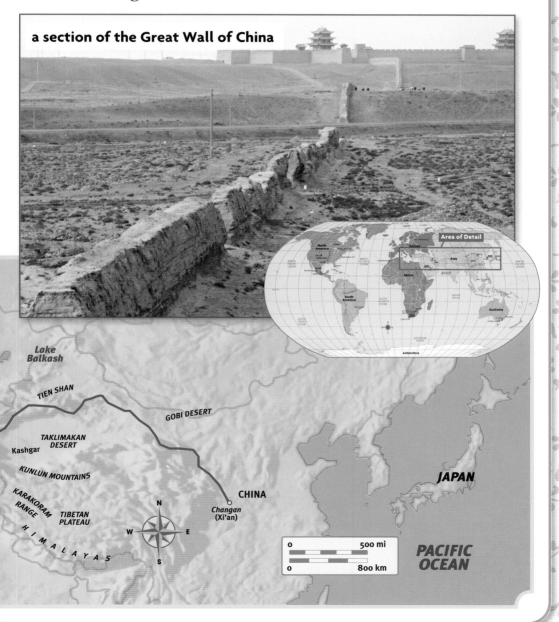

a section of the Great Wall of China

A HIGHWAY FOR THE AGES

The year is 200 C.E. In Capua, Italy, a town 130 miles (209 kilometers) south of Rome, General Marcus Avellinus is having dinner at home, surrounded by friends and family.

"I want to show you something I bought at the marketplace in Rome," the general tells them. He holds up a thin, shimmering, bright red material. No one at the dinner has ever seen a cloth like this before. They all stare at it in amazement.

"What kind of cloth is this, Marcus?" one of them asks. "It appears to have been spun on the looms of the gods!"

People shopping at a vegetable market outside Roman Emperor Diocletian's palace around 300 C.E.

"Philemon, the glass merchant who sold it to me, called it silk," the general replies. "Neither he nor anyone in the marketplace knows how it is made. Philemon brought it back from a place called Samarkand. The man who sold it to him claimed it comes from the farthest reaches of the Earth."

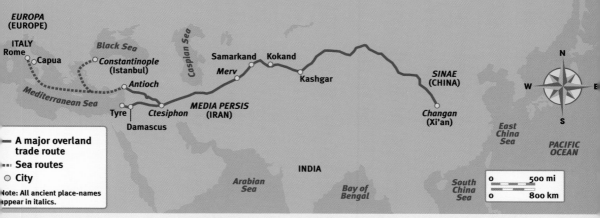

the Silk Road, first century C.E.

At the same time, thousands of miles away, in the Chinese city of Changan, a trader named Wun Li has just returned home from a year-long journey. He had traveled westward to the markets of Samarkand to trade silk made in China for goods from other lands.

Wun Li runs excitedly up the street to the home of Wang Po, the nobleman who sent him on the silk-trading quest. He is careful not to jostle the precious package he is carrying. It contains the most exotic object he found in the marketplace.

Wun Li's hands shake as he removes a small, clear bottle from a cloth bag. He gives it to Wang Po, who holds it up to the light.

"What is this?" says Wang Po, his eyes wide with wonder. "It is a bottle, to be sure, but I can see through it!"

Wun Li knows that he has brought back something special. He smiles proudly. "The merchant who bought a great deal of the silk sold it to me," says Wun Li. "He called it glass. He says it was made in his distant homeland."

Venetian glass with enamel decorations from around 1300 C.E.

Spanning the Known World

Silk from China and glass from Europe were only two of the many kinds of goods that traveled the Silk Road. Ivory, metalwork, horses, and more came from Europe and the Middle East. Tea, paper, and ceramics came from the East. Spices, furs, jade, gold, and silver came from both directions to be traded. By far the most important **commodity** was silk. It was so precious that it became the main form of currency. The world's longest trade route of the time even bore the name of this prized product.

But objects weren't the only things traded on the Silk Road. Ideas, stories, cultural traditions, and beliefs were exchanged as well. The Chinese learned glassblowing and winemaking from the West. The Europeans learned papermaking, printing, and silk production from the East. Religions also spread along the Silk Road. Buddhism moved east to China from India. Judaism, Christianity, and Islam spread eastward from the Mediterranean Sea. Confucianism spread westward from China. **Zoroastrianism** spread westward from Central Asia.

Traveling the Silk Road

Hardly anyone ever traveled the whole length of the Silk Road. Instead, merchants brought their goods part of the way and traded them. Those same goods were then brought by other travelers to another part of the road and traded, and so on. It was like a long relay race, except that things traveled very slowly. In fact, it would take at least a year for anything to complete the journey between China and Europe.

a modern-day camel caravan in Afghanistan

Anyone who set out on the Silk Road had to be prepared for a perilous journey. The roads crossed huge deserts and icy mountain ranges. Robbers and warring armies would attack the traders, steal their goods, and sometimes kill the travelers. For protection, merchants traveled in huge groups called caravans. Camels were the main means of transportation. One camel could carry about 1,100 pounds (500 kilograms) of goods at a time and go for two weeks without water. Some caravans were 1,000 camels long! Merchants often walked alongside their beasts of burden in order to get the most goods possible on their camels' backs.

Caravans moved very slowly, about 2½ miles (4 kilometers) an hour. They usually traveled at night to avoid the brutal heat of the day. Night travel made it easier to evade possible attackers, too. It was hundreds of miles between major cities and towns on the Silk Road. So every 30 or 40 miles (48 or 64 kilometers), the length of a day's journey, the caravans would stop at inns called **caravanserais**. There the merchants could find shelter and the animals could rest.

Until the advent of computers and the Internet centuries later, the Silk Road and the camel remained, arguably, the most important means of international exchange throughout history.

HISTORY'S AMAZING CLOTH

Ateam of Canadian chemists stares intently at the milky white liquid in a glass container. This is it. After years of experimenting, they believe they have discovered a way to make a cloth that is lighter than cotton but stronger than steel. A member of the team uses tweezers to pull the first delicate thread from the liquid. The thread is the kind made from a spider's glands. The liquid is goat's milk. The scientists have combined the genes of two completely different creatures to make a revolutionary new fabric. And they couldn't have done it without the help of 5,000 years of Chinese knowledge. The chemists have created twenty-first-century silk. But it was the Chinese who discovered silk first.

A Secret Treasure

Most **anthropologists** believe that silk was first produced in China around 2700 B.C.E. No one knows who first thought of it, but someone must have been paying close attention to the white, fluffy cocoons woven by the *Bombyx mori* (bahm-BIKS MOR-ee) moth. That person must have been impressed by the cocoons' softness and strength. Deciding to use those cocoons to make cloth was an ingenious idea.

From the time silk cloth was created, it was a fabulous sight. Silk shimmered in the sun. It was strong yet lightweight.

The material was so highly prized that it was traded all the way from China to Rome and became a form of currency. People traded silk for horses and slaves. Leaders of armies paid their soldiers in silk. Kings even used it to settle peace treaties.

No one outside of China could figure out how silk was made. Some people thought it came directly from the leaves of trees. Others thought it was collected from the soft under-feathers of birds! Ammianus Marcellinus (am-ee-AY-nus mar-suh-LY-nus), a Roman historian in the fourth century B.C.E., declared, "Silk fabrics are made from soil. Chinese soil is soft as wool. After watering and special **cultivation**, it can be used for silk thread formation." Silk production was such a highly kept secret that anyone who smuggled out the cocoons or moths was put to death.

Eventually the secret of silk was discovered, and other countries began to **manufacture** it. India and Japan led the way, followed by the Middle East. By the fifteenth century, Europeans were making their own silk.

How Traditional Silk Is Made

The basic process of making traditional silk hasn't changed for thousands of years. The *Bombyx mori* moth starts out as an egg the size of a grain of rice. In eight to ten days, it hatches as a very tiny worm called a larva. The larva, or silkworm, does nothing but eat. And it eats only one kind of food: the leaves of a mulberry tree. By the time it is fully grown three weeks later, the silkworm is 10,000 times heavier! It is now a bulky caterpillar, about the size of a human little finger, with enough strength to build a cocoon.

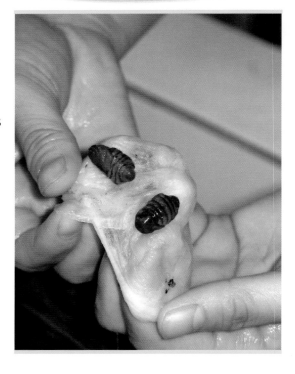

Inside the cocoon, the silkworm slowly changes into a moth. To make its cocoon, the silkworm attaches itself to a tree branch and begins to ooze out a gummy liquid from a gland under its lower lip. As the liquid hits the air, it starts to dry into a thread. The silkworm twists and moves its head from side to side, wrapping the thread around its entire body. It will move its head about 24,000 times over four days. The completed cocoon is one single thread 2,000 to 3,000 feet (610 to 914 meters) long!

Breeding silkworms and harvesting their cocoons is called **sericulture**. In ancient China, only women worked in the sericulture industry. They would gather moths and mulberry leaves. (It takes the leaves of four mulberry trees to produce one pound of silk.) Once the cocoons were formed, they would be placed in boiling water to kill the silkworm caterpillar inside. Then each cocoon was unwound carefully in order not to tangle or break the thread. All of this was done by hand.

Modern Silk Production

Today, silk production is mechanized in large factories. The silkworm larvae are kept in containers at a constant temperature between 65°F and 77°F (18°C to 25°C). They are fed mulberry leaves every half hour around the clock. Care is taken to keep the area quiet and away from any breeze or unusual smell that would frighten the larvae.

China, India, and Japan produce most of the world's silk. In India alone, at least eleven universities have sericulture departments to study silk production. In 2008, Japanese scientists discovered that adding a jasminelike scent to the silkworm's food speeds up the silk production cycle.

Other scientists have been inspired by traditional silk making. They are now finding ways to produce silk using bees and even spiders. The Canadian researchers who combined spider and goat genes have produced a thread that is incredibly thin and strong. Such silk can be used to sew stitches during brain and eye surgeries. It can be mixed with paint to coat boats and space stations. It can also be woven to make bulletproof vests and even cables that hold up bridges!

Silkworms feed on mulberry leaves.

Silk making has a long, cherished history. As today's scientists continue and expand upon that tradition, they will continue to discover new, extraordinary uses for this amazing thread.

Analyze the Information in the Articles

- What are the articles about?
- What do the two articles have in common?
- How are the articles different?
- Both articles contained graphics such as photographs and illustrations. How do these features help you understand the articles?
- How did each article end?

Focus on Comprehension: Draw Conclusions

Use the first article to answer the first two questions. Use the second article to answer the third question.

- What can you conclude about the Silk Road and the items that were traded on it?
- People who traveled the Silk Road had to be tough. How can you tell?
- Reread "How Traditional Silk Is Made" and "Modern Silk Production." (pages 13–15) What can you conclude about the process of making silk?

Analyze the Tools Writers Use: Strong Lead

- Look at the lead in the articles. What types of leads did the author use? Direct or indirect? How can you tell?
- Compare the two leads. The first lead is long while the second lead is short. Which lead did you prefer? Or did you like both of them the same? Why?
- What did you expect to learn after reading the leads?

Focus on Words: Word Origins

Make a chart like the one below. Locate each word in the book. Use a dictionary or the Internet to identify the word's origin and its history, such as when it was first used and by whom. Finally, write a definition for the word.

Page	Word	Word Origins	Word History	Definition
10	commodity			
10	Zoroastrianism			
11	caravanserais			
12	anthropologists			
13	cultivation			
13	manufacture			
14	sericulture			

HUNZA: THE LAND THAT TIME FORGOT

W e're almost there!" English guide Roger Markham calls out to his group of western tourists. Their small van is slowly descending southward on a side road of the Karakoram (kar-uh-KOR-um) Highway in northern Pakistan. "Can you hear the music? The wedding celebration has begun!"

The sound of drums, flutes, and stringed instruments wafts upward from Altit, their afternoon destination. The tourists are going to attend a local wedding feast. But they will also feel like they have traveled back in time thousands of years. The Hunza region they are in runs along the ancient northern Silk Road. It is a land that time forgot.

As the van enters Altit, the town's children greet the tourists. They run alongside the van, laughing and waving. Half the year, it is very snowy and cold in the Hunza Valley, and tourists are rare. But now it is early autumn, and the tourists are back.

The Hunzakuts welcome the tourists to their celebration. They are poor but very **hospitable** people. Far from being **xenophobic**, they are eager to share their culture with others.

The women are preparing a wedding feast of mutton, dried apricots, yogurt, a flat bread called *chupati*, and newly pressed grape wine. A group of old men are already dancing. They lift their swords high, kick their legs, twirl, and twist.

A Hunzakut woman gathers grain in the fields of Altit.

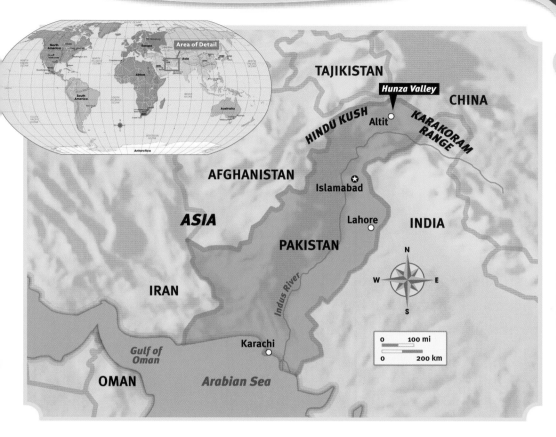

"They are like acrobats!" says one astonished tourist.

Markham smiles. "That's because they've had lots of practice. You see, most of them are **centenarians**."

In Eastern literature, there are tales of a place called Shangri-la. It is a fantasy world high in the mountains, where people live to be hundreds of years old. Some people believe that Hunza was the inspiration for Shangri-la. It is quite common for a Hunzakut to reach the age of 100. After much study, **gerontologists** and other scientists now believe they know why.

One of the factors is heredity: Hunzakuts have certain genes that increase their life expectancy. Whereas Westerners' average life span is somewhere between seventy-five and eighty, the Hunzakuts' average is ninety years old.

Hunza: The Land That Time Forgot

But biology is only a small part of it. The Hunzakut lifestyle really makes a difference. For one thing, Hunza is surrounded by huge mountain ranges. Year-round glaciers provide some of the purest drinking water in the world. The water has a white tint and contains minerals that keep the local people healthy. The Hunzakut call it glacier milk.

In terraces cut into the steep lands, Hunzakut farmers grow cherry, apricot, and apple trees. In the valleys they grow buckwheat, millet, and lots of vegetables. They don't use pesticides on their crops or preservatives in their food. They herd sheep and goats for their milk, from which they make cheese, butter, and yogurt. They rarely eat meat. And they eat about thirty percent less per day than do most westerners. No one is overweight. That explains why cancer and heart disease are rare among them.

Schoolgirls walk along a trail next to terraced gardens in the Hunza Valley.

Moreover, the people in this region lead stress-free lives. They work very hard—twelve hours a day, seven days a week—and live in stone and wooden houses; most have little or no electricity. But they are a peaceful, happy people. The women weave beautiful wool rugs, shawls, and hats to sell to tourists. The men make silver and gold jewelry and fine wooden furniture.

For centuries, Hunza was a remote region. That all began to change in the 1960s and 1970s when the Karakoram Highway was built connecting Pakistan and China. Some Hunza cities along the highway began to be influenced

a silversmith in his shop in Karimabad, in northern Pakistan

by more modern culture. Along with electricity, TV sets, and computers, Hunzakuts have been exposed to poorer diets. As a result, some Hunzakuts are now developing heart disease and cancer and are not living as long.

Such changes are worrisome. Will Hunzakuts be able to preserve their way of life? Can the rest of the world learn valuable lessons from them before their ways vanish? What will become of this modern-day Shangri-la? In the land that time forgot, it seems that only time will tell.

BUILDING A 21ST-CENTURY SILK ROAD

As soon as you enter the East Gate of the city of Kashgar, China, your senses are assaulted by the bright colors of Turkish scarves and Iranian rugs; the sweet aromas of cinnamon, ginger, and cloves; and all the raucous noises that make up the old Grand Sunday Bazaar. A camel seller urges a reluctant buyer to take an animal for a test drive. Three women argue with a fruit seller about the freshness of his melons. Children run among the 100,000 people that shop at the 5,000 booths in this marketplace. The chaotic bargaining activities can be overwhelming to anyone not native to the city.

For more than 2,000 years, Kashgar was a major crossroads on the Silk Road. Its bazaar was known as the largest fair in Asia. In some ways, the market looks the same today as it did in the first century B.C.E. But on closer inspection, one can see that the twenty-first century has arrived. Some booths contain electronics: radios, TVs, and CD players. Others have used motorcycles. Still others display small appliances and even kitchen sinks. Clearly, the Silk Road has endured— and changed. What has led to this **transformation**?

at the Sunday Bazaar in Kashgar, China

A Highway Across Asia

Today a modern Silk Road has risen amid the deserts and snow-covered mountains from Western Europe to China. It is called the Asian Highway. This network of eighty-three routes covers more than 91,000 miles (147,000 kilometers). That's thirteen times longer than the original Silk Road! The idea to construct such a major transportation system dates back to 1959, when Asian countries began to grow prosperous. The nations in this area saw a way to improve their trade and tourism by expanding on the idea of the old Silk Road.

The writer presents facts about the new transportation system that is underway.

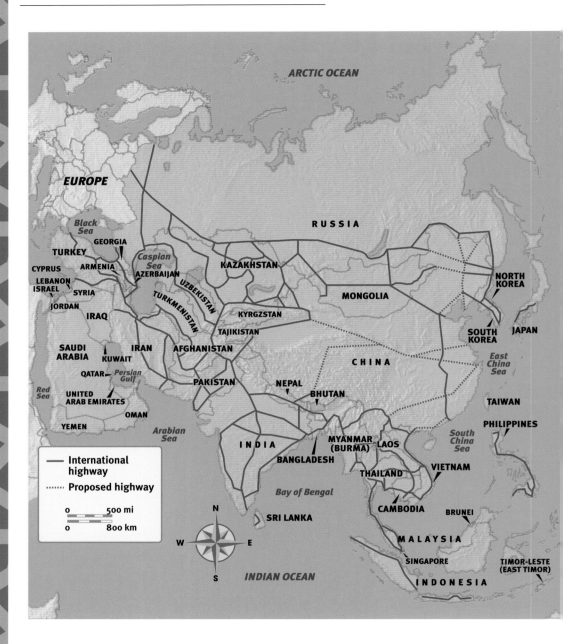

In the 1960s and 1970s, the countries worked on plans to link their existing roads and form even more connections. Building the highway network would involve a total of thirty-two countries and cost about $44 billion.

In 1992, the plans were finally in place, and the United Nations created the Asian Highway project. In 2003, an international agreement was created for the countries to sign. Everyone had to agree to build their roads the same way so that drivers anywhere could travel easily and without confusion. As scholar and researcher Sanjoy Hazarika said at the time, "The Asian Highway project requires collective effort and close collaboration among the Asian countries." It took about five years for all thirty-two governments to agree to the terms of the contract.

The writer provides a primary source quote from a scholar who is an expert on Asia. The quote supports the writer's opinion that the project is a major undertaking.

Controversies Over Construction

Getting thirty-two countries to agree on the same plans was a difficult thing. Some countries such as India, Russia, China, and Japan are large, wealthy, and powerful, and they already have highways of their own. Other countries such as Armenia, Cambodia, Bhutan, and Nepal are small, poor, remote, and they lack even basic paved roads. How would the costs be shared? Whose highway would link to whose, and where?

A different issue existed between Bangladesh and India. The two countries have a history of tense relations. But India raised little objection to the new highway, since it had had access to old highways that crossed through Bangladesh when it was still part of Pakistan. Bangladesh was worried about its national security.

The text is logically organized: The writer first states that getting countries to agree on the project was difficult, and then she provides examples. She follows with another controversial issue.

In 1965, India and Pakistan were at war. After the war, the country of Bangladesh was created. The Bangladeshi government didn't want to sign the agreement if it meant that India might be able to send cars, trucks, and perhaps even military vehicles into its territories. It was also afraid that India would have easier access to markets that Bangladesh relied on to support its economy. Finally, Bangladesh agreed to join the Asian Highway. Its doing so would allow Bangladeshi products to travel much shorter routes to China and gain many more customers.

Yet another issue has to do with how the Asian Highway will affect the environment. One part of the network, a 1,600-mile (2,600-kilometer) road called the Mongolian Millennium Highway, will connect China and Mongolia. It will go through a vast section of grassland that is home to herds of endangered gazelles.

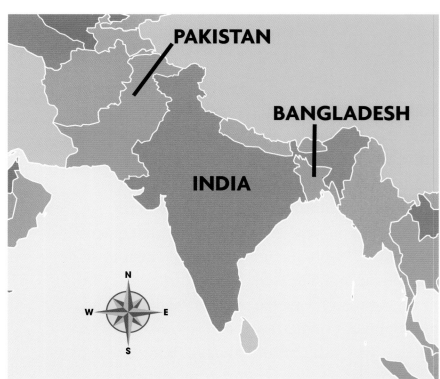

Scientists from the Wildlife **Conservation** Society are concerned that the road will ruin the gazelles' habitat. They are protesting the plans. They are looking for a more environmentally friendly route, one that will meet the needs of both people and gazelles.

The writer presents another perspective on the highway: Conservationists are concerned about the destruction that will result from this progress.

When the Asian Highway is complete, it will travel through areas where sixty percent of the world's population lives. Is it a success so far? Just ask the people at the old Grand Sunday Bazaar. Since 1992, it has been held every day, not just on Sundays. Lately it's gotten a new name: the International Trade Market of Central and Western Asia. It looks like Kashgar has entered the twenty-first century.

The writer's strong ending will keep readers thinking about the places mentioned in the piece, the highway project, and the changes brought about by progress.

Tibetan gazelles

27

Analyze the Information in the Articles

- What are the articles about?
- The book's theme is the Silk Road. How do these articles match the theme?
- What is the author's purpose for these articles?
- Both articles contain graphics such as photographs and maps. How do these features help you understand the articles?
- How does each article end?

Focus on Comprehension: Draw Conclusions

Use the first article to answer the first question. Use the second article to answer the last two questions.

- What can you conclude about the Hunzakut diet?
- Reread "A Highway Across Asia." Building a highway over millions of miles takes a lot of time. How can you tell?
- Reread "Controversies Over Construction." What can you conclude about the countries involved in this massive project?

A vendor at the Kashgar Market

Analyze the Tools Writers Use: Strong Lead

- The author uses indirect leads in both articles.
  Explain how.
- Compare the two leads. How are they the similar?
  How are they different?
- What did you expect to learn after reading the leads?

Focus on Words: Word Origins

Make a chart like the one below. Locate each word in the book. Use a dictionary or the Internet to identify the word's origin and its history, such as when it was first used and by whom. Finally, write a definition of the word.

Page	Word	Word Origins	Word History	Definition
18	hospitable			
18	xenophobic			
19	centenarians			
19	gerontologists			
23	transformation			
27	conservation			

How does an author write an INFORMATIONAL TEXT?

Reread "Building a 21st-Century Silk Road" and think about what Jeanette Leardi did to write this informational text. How did she keep a narrow focus? How did she help you understand the text?

① Decide on a topic.
Choose something you are interested in and want to know more about. Good writers enjoy researching their topics.

② Narrow your focus.
Jeanette Leardi knew she couldn't include everything there is to know about the Asian Highway project, so she narrowed her focus to some of the issues surrounding its construction.

③ Write a question about your focus.
Questions lead to answers, so turn your focus into a question.

④ Research your focus.
Become the expert by reading articles on the Internet, reading books and newspaper articles, and interviewing people connected with your topic. For instance, Jeanette corresponded with a scholar and expert on Asia. You want to show readers that you know what you are talking about.

⑤ Organize your information.
Before writing an informational text, make a chart or table like the one on the next page that outlines the main points. For each main point, identify supporting details. You don't have to write full sentences. These are your notes. Remember, however, that there should be a logical progression of ideas.

⑥ Write your informational text.
As you write, develop each main point with your supporting details. Remember, you want people to enjoy reading your article as well as to learn something new.

Topic: **Asian Highway project**

Focus: **Construction Issues**

Question: **What are some of the issues that must be dealt with to get the highway built?**

Main Point	Details
Introduction	Construction of the Asian Highway network, an important transportation system, is underway. It will make travel easier and bring modern ways to some remote areas like Kashgar, China.
Thirty-two nations are participating.	All countries had to agree to build their roads the same way to make traveling seamless. It took five years for all thirty-two governments to agree to details.
An issue existed between India and Bangladesh.	Because of a history of tense relations between Bangladesh and Pakistan, Bangladesh was worried about its national security. Bangladesh eventually agreed to participate.
An environmental issue exists.	One 1,600-mile section of highway will pass through grasslands inhabited by an endangered species of gazelle. Environmentalists are protesting and demanding a route change.
Conclusion	The project is nearing completion. The bazaar in Kashgar is already realizing the benefits. It has more modern goods and is open every day.

Glossary

anthropologist   (an-thruh-PAH-luh-jist) someone who studies human beings (page 12)

caravanserais   (kair-uh-VAN-suh-reez) inns in eastern countries where caravans used to rest (page 11)

centenarian   (sen-teh-NAIR-ee-un) a person who is 100 years old or more (page 19)

commodity   (kuh-MAH-dih-tee) a product that is traded (page 10)

conservation   (kahn-ser-VAY-shun) protection of plants and animals (page 27)

cultivation   (kul-tih-VAY-shun) preparing land for farming (page 13)

gerontologist   (jair-un-TAH-luh-jist) a person who studies the elderly (page 19)

hospitable   (hah-SPIH-tuh-bul) welcoming to guests (page 18)

manufacture   (man-yuh-FAK-cher) to produce (page 13)

sericulture   (SAIR-ih-kul-cher) raising silkworms to make silk (page 14)

transformation   (trans-fer-MAY-shun) changing one thing into another (page 23)

xenophobic   (zeh-nuh-FOH-bik) afraid of foreigners (page 18)

Zoroastrianism   (zor-uh-WAS-tree-uh-nih-zum) a Persian religion that was founded in the sixth century B.C.E. (page 10)